D0483917

LETTERS
by a Modern Mystic

Excerpts from letters written to his father by
Frank C. Laubach

purposeful design®
p u b l i c a t i o n s
Colorado Springs, Colorado

Purposeful Design Publications is the publishing division of the Association of
Christian Schools International (ACSI) and is committed to the ministry of
Christian school education, to enable Christian educators and schools worldwide to
effectively prepare students for life. As the publisher of textbooks, trade books, and
other educational resources within ACSI, Purposeful Design Publications strives to
produce biblically sound materials that reflect Christian scholarship and stewardship
and that address the identified needs of Christian schools around the world.

Unless otherwise identified, all Scripture quotations are taken from the Holy
Bible, New International Version® (NIV®), © 1973, 1978, 1984 by International
Bible Society. All rights reserved worldwide. The "NIV" and "New International
Version" are trademarks registered in the United States Patent and Trademark
Office by International Bible Society. Use of either trademark requires the
permission of International Bible Society.

Excerpts of *The Game with Minutes* were originally published by SeedSowers
Publishing House, Jacksonville, FL, in the book *Practicing His Presence* by Brother
Lawrence and Frank Laubach. Used with permission.

Printed in Mexico
12 11 10 09 08 07   3 4 5 6 7

Library of Congress Cataloging-in-Publication Data
Laubach, Frank Charles, 1884-1970.
Letters by a modern mystic: excerpts from letters written to his
father / by Frank C. Laubach.
    p. cm.
  ISBN 978-1-58331-091-5
  1. Mysticism. I. Title.
BV5085.L3 2007
248.2'2--dc22
                              2007036757

Purposeful Design Publications Catalog # 6326

Editorial team: Gina Brandon and Karen Friesen
Design: Michael Riester
Cover image: Robert Redelowski

Purposeful Design Publications
A Division of ACSI
PO Box 65130 • Colorado Springs, CO 80962-5130
Customer Service: 800/367-0798 • Website: www.acsi.org

CONTENTS

FROM PURPOSEFUL DESIGN PUBLICATIONS

BY STEVE BABBITT, DIRECTOR, PUBLISHING SERVICES

Letters by a Modern Mystic was first published in 1937. Since that initial publication, it has been reprinted at least twenty-one times. Until this 2007 printing, the most recent was in 1984 on the 100th anniversary of Frank Laubach's birth.

The Game with Minutes, included after *Letters*, was written in the 1930s by Frank Laubach to be a practical guide for those who wanted to "put into practice" the principles articulated by *Letters*.

In Purposeful Design Publications' pursuit to publish *Letters by a Modern Mystic*, I have had the honor of establishing a long-distance friendship with Dr. Robert S. Laubach, the son of Frank C. Laubach. He has been most gracious in our conversations, and his enthusiasm to have the work of his father brought to life again is overwhelming. Purposeful Design Publications is deeply grateful to Bob Laubach for the privilege granted to us.

FOREWORD

BY DALLAS WILLARD

You hold in your hands a treasure provided by Christ to all people who long to live their real life today in the constant presence and power of God. It comes through the soul of a man who lived such a life—Frank Laubach. He was a quintessentially modern man, totally at home in world affairs at all levels, but in all contexts the constant servant of Christ and of his fellow human beings. An international statesman for Christ, Laubach had the most profound simplicity, intelligence, and spirituality. As you will find, the man himself is even greater than his message. He himself is the assurance that what he says about a constant life with God and in God is true.

What Frank Laubach brings to us, with his poetic imagery and limpid prose, is a simple and effectual way into a life in which God is always near and all of the intimacies and empowerments extolled in Scripture and in hymns and other praise songs form the texture of daily life. In a way well known to Christ followers of other times but largely lost to followers of more recent forms of Christianity, he shows us the simple, practical steps that we can take—no matter our "qualifications" or circumstances—to fill our minds with the reality of God, of Christ, and of His Kingdom.

The method is simple, and it can be learned with some sustained practice in such a way that it is not a burden but a blessing that gives much more strength than it requires. In the briefest of descriptions, we learn "to call Him to mind at least one second of each minute." We practice this, learning as we go, until it is as routine as breathing. Then our life is flooded with light and joy and strength for all that is good. Other things are helpful, such as periodic, intense study of the Gospels and fellowship with others who are walking the same way and practicing the same life. But the heart of the matter is turning the mind to God for one brief second of each minute. When we set ourselves to do this, we will discover many ways of doing it and many things that can help us. God will assist the eager soul to learn as it goes.

Frank Laubach was well educated in how the mind works. He knew how we are capable of keeping many things before the mind at once, and he knew that when something is drawn before the mind it does not disappear immediately. Rather, it lingers around the mind, and the fragrance of its being stains the atmosphere of consciousness. So God and His works are always there, from horizon to center.

Anyone who wants to actively love God all the time can do this. A child can do it, as well as those who have no special qualifications or advantages. If you will patiently begin to follow the instructions given in this book, you will very quickly see the astonishing results. Why not begin now? The door is open, and the Master calls. You certainly have nothing better to do. As you follow these instructions, everything else you do will go better than ever before.

Dallas Willard

INTRODUCTION

BY KEN SMITHERMAN

I have often contemplated Jesus' directive in Matthew 28:19: "Therefore go and make disciples." My contemplation has been in regard to what it takes to make disciples. Disciple making is about teaching. And teaching—at least effective teaching—requires some things of significance. During my pursuit of that thought, I was reading Dallas Willard's *The Great Omission*, which drew my attention to the life and work of Frank C. Laubach, a missionary. As a matter of fact, I was so intrigued by Willard's writing about Laubach that I began seeking a copy of his book *Letters by a Modern Mystic* (1937), which consists of excerpts from letters that Laubach began writing in 1930 when he was a lonely missionary serving on the island of Mindanao in the Philippines.

I was very captivated by Frank Laubach's personal sensitivity in his letters to his father. He wrote, "Although I have been a minister and a missionary for fifteen years, I have not lived the entire day of every day in minute-by-minute effort to follow the will of God. Two years ago a profound dissatisfaction led me to begin trying to line up my actions with the will of God.... But this year I have started out trying to live all my waking moments in conscious listening to the inner voice, asking without ceasing, 'What, Father, do you desire said? What, Father, do you desire done this minute?' "

As I read, I thought this way of living just might be the essence of critical steps in the pursuit of genuine discipleship and spiritual formation. I became powerfully moved by the Holy Spirit regarding the impact that living this way could have on individuals, families, churches, schools, entire communities, cultures—the world. Although these letters were written nearly eighty years ago, they speak forcefully to anyone who desires the highest level of the pursuit of God and effective discipleship and discipling.

After discovering that the book had been published several times but was currently out of print, Purposeful Design Publications began the process of gaining permission to publish excerpts from Frank Laubach's letters. We established contact with Robert Laubach, his son. Robert remains active with ProLiteracy Worldwide, continuing the adult literacy program that his father began as an expansion of his Kingdom service. ProLiteracy Worldwide has helped millions of illiterate adults around the world learn to read. We are especially grateful to Dr. Robert Laubach for his gracious permission and enthusiastic support for this publication of excerpts from his father's letters and *The Game with Minutes*. May you find this book challenging and particularly encouraging. It is one man's testimony of life in an intentional moment-by-moment relationship with the Heavenly Father.

Ken Smitherman, President
Association of Christian Schools International

A Son Introducing His Father

Why read a diary kept by a man who lived three-quarters of a century ago? Because it is a diary of a man's walk with God. That man—Frank C. Laubach, my father—kept this diary at a time when his life was at its most discouraging depth.

He was alone in an alien land, among a people whose language he had yet to learn and whose religion he had yet to appreciate. Their indifference rebuffed this missionary, who was so well trained and so eager to help them. In despair, he spoke with God night after night on Signal Hill, a convenient knoll just outside the town of Dansalan in the Philippines.

As this prayer diary tells, he gradually learned to talk and to walk with God. As he did so, God humbled him and taught him to walk and work with his new Maranao friends. From this spiritual journey emerged the unique concept of God's love in action expressed by a literate person teaching an illiterate person.

Anyone who understands the spiritual depth on which "each one teach one" rests should return frequently to this little book.

Robert S. Laubach
Syracuse, New York, September 2007

THE LETTERS

DANSALAN • LAKE LANAO, PHILIPPINES

3 JANUARY 1930

To be able to look backward and say, "This, *this* has been the finest year of my life"—that is glorious! But anticipation! To be able to look ahead and say, "The present year can and *shall* be better!"—that is more glorious!

If we said such things about our achievements, we would be consummate egotists. But if we are speaking of God's kindness, and we speak truly, we are but grateful. And this is what I do witness. I have done nothing but open windows—God has done all the rest. There have been few if any conspicuous achievements. There has been a succession of marvelous experiences of the friendship of God. I feel, as I look back over the year, that it would have been impossible to have held much more without breaking with sheer joy. It was the lonesomest year, in some ways the hardest year, of my life, but the most gloriously full of voices from heaven.

And it closed very beautifully. The young men and girls of Silliman were gathered for a watch night service. We were resolving new high resolves until nearly twelve o'clock.

As for me, I resolved that I would succeed better this year with my experiment of filling every minute full of the thought of God than I succeeded last year.

And I added another resolve—to be as wide open toward people and their need as I am toward God. Windows open outward as well as upward! Windows *especially* open downward where people need most!

Living in the atmosphere of Islam is proving—thus far—a tremendous spiritual stimulus. Mohammed is helping me. I have no more intention of giving up Christianity and becoming a Mohammedan than I had twenty years ago, but I find myself richer for the Islamic experience of God.

Islam stresses the *will* of God. It is supreme. We cannot alter any of His mighty decrees. To try to do so means annihilation. Submission is the first and last duty of man.

That is exactly what I have been needing in my Christian life. Although I have been a minister and a missionary for fifteen years, I have not lived the entire day of every day in minute-by-minute effort to follow the will of God. Two years ago a profound dissatisfaction led me to begin trying to line up my actions with the will of God about every fifteen minutes or every half hour. Other people to whom I confessed this intention said it was impossible. I judge from what I have heard that few people are really trying even that.

But this year I have started out trying to live all my waking moments in conscious listening to the inner voice, asking without ceasing, "What, Father, do you desire said? What, Father, do you desire done this minute?"

It is clear that this is exactly what Jesus was doing all day every day. But it is not what His followers have been doing in very large numbers.

26 JANUARY 1930

You who will read these letters will know that I am here exploring two lands which for me are new. One of them is within my own soul; the other is in the soul of the Moros.

For the past few days I have been experimenting in a more complete surrender than ever before. I am taking, by deliberate act of will, enough time from each hour to give God much thought. Yesterday and today I have made a new adventure, which is not easy to express. I am feeling God in each movement, by an act of will—willing that He shall direct these fingers that now strike this typewriter—willing that He shall pour through my steps as I walk—willing that He shall direct my words as I speak, and my very jaws as I eat!

You will object to this intense introspection. Do not try it, unless you feel dissatisfied with your own relationship with God, but at least allow me to realize all the leadership of God I can. I am disgusted with the pettiness and futility of my unled self. If the way out is not more perfect slavery to

God, then what is the way out? Paul speaks of our liberty in Christ. I am trying to be utterly free from everybody, free from my own self, but completely enslaved to the will of God every moment of this day.

We used to sing a song in the church of my boyhood in Benton, which I liked, but which I never really practiced until now. It runs:

> Moment by moment, I'm kept in His love;
> Moment by moment, I've life from above;
> Looking to Jesus till glory doth shine;
> Moment by moment, O Lord, I am Thine.

It is exactly that "moment by moment," every waking moment, surrender, responsiveness, obedience, sensitiveness, pliability, "lost in His love," that I now have the mind-bent to explore with all my might. It means two burning passions: First, to be like Jesus. Second, to respond to God as a violin responds to the bow of the master.

In defense of my opening my soul and laying it bare to the public gaze in this fashion, I may say that it seems to me that we really seldom do anybody much good except as we share the deepest experiences of our souls in this way. It is not the fashion to tell your inmost thoughts, but there are many wrong fashions, and concealment of the best in us is wrong. I disapprove of the usual practice of talking "small talk" whenever we meet, and holding a veil over our souls. If we are so impoverished that we have nothing to reveal but small talk, then we need to struggle for more richness of soul. As for me, I am convinced that this spiritual pilgrimage which I am making is infinitely worthwhile, the most important thing I know of to talk about. And talk I shall while there is anybody to listen. And I hunger—O how I hunger! for others to tell me their soul adventures.

Outside the window, as I completed the last page, has been one of the most splendorous sunsets I have ever seen. And these words came singing through my soul, "Looking to Jesus 'till glory doth shine!" Glory had been shining all across the sky until everything was crimson. Even the paper on which I was writing became red with the reflection from the roseate sky. It was the reflection of my own soul where God had today been painting His wonderful visions. Is not this marvelous sky a parable! Open your soul and entertain the glory of God and after a while that glory will be reflected in the world about you and in the very clouds above your head.

29 JANUARY 1930

DANSALAN • LAKE LANAO, PHILIPPINES

I feel simply carried along each hour, doing my part in a plan which is far beyond myself. This sense of cooperation with God in little things is what so astonishes me, for I never have felt it this way before. I need something, and turn round to find it waiting for me. I must work, to be sure, but there is God working along with me. To know this gives a sense of security and assurance for the future which is also new to my life. I seem to have to make sure of only one thing now, and every other thing "takes care of itself," or I prefer to say what is more true, God takes care of all the rest. My part is to *live this hour in continuous inner conversation with God and in perfect responsiveness to His will, to make this hour gloriously rich.* This seems to be all I need think about.

DANSALAN · LAKE LANAO · PHILIPPINES

1 MARCH 1930

The sense of being led by an unseen hand which takes mine while another hand reaches ahead and prepares the way, grows upon me daily. I do not need to strain at all to find opportunity. It plies in upon me as the waves roll over the beach, and yet there is time to do something about each opportunity.

Perhaps a man who has been an ordained minister since 1914 ought to be ashamed to confess that he never before felt the joy of complete hourly, minute by minute—now what shall I call it?—more than surrender. I had that before. More than listening to God. I tried that before. I cannot find the word that will mean to you or to me what I am now experiencing. It is a will act. I compel my mind to open straight out toward God. I wait and listen with determined sensitiveness. I fix my attention there, and sometimes it requires a long time early in the morning to attain that mental state. I determine not to get out of bed until that mind set, that concentration upon God, is settled. It also requires determination to keep it there, for I feel as though the words and thoughts of others near me were constantly exerting a drag backward or sidewise. But for the most part recently I have not lost sight of this purpose for long and have soon come back to it. After a while, perhaps, it will become a habit, and the sense of effort will grow less.

But why do I constantly harp upon this inner experience? Because I feel convinced that for me and for you who read there lie ahead undiscovered continents of spiritual living compared with which we are infants in arms.

And I must witness that people outside are treating me differently. Obstacles which I once would have regarded as insurmountable are melting away like a mirage. People are becoming friendly who suspected or neglected me. I feel, I *feel* like one who has had his violin out of tune with the orchestra and at last is in harmony with the music of the universe.

As for me, I never lived, I was half dead, I was a rotting tree, until I reached the place where I wholly, with utter honesty, resolved and then re-resolved that I *would* find God's will, and I *would* do that will though every fiber in me said no, and I *would* win the battle in my thoughts. It was as though some deep artesian well had been struck in my soul and strength came forth. I do not claim success even for a day yet, in my mind, not complete success all day, but some days are close to success, and every day is tingling with the joy of a glorious discovery. That thing is eternal. That thing is undefeatable. You and I shall soon blow away from our bodies. Money, praise, poverty, opposition, these make no difference, for they will all alike be forgotten in a thousand years, but this spirit which comes to a mind set upon continuous surrender, this spirit is timeless life.

9
MARCH
1930

For the first time in my life I know what I must do off in lonesome Lanao. I know why God left this aching void, for Himself to fill. Off on this mountain I must do three things:

1. I must pursue this voyage of discovery in quest of God's will. I must because the world needs me to do it.

2. I must plunge into mighty experiments in intercessory prayer, to test my hypothesis that God needs my help to do His will for others, and that my prayer releases His power. I must be His channel, for the world needs me.

3. I must confront these Moros with a divine love which will speak Christ to them though I never use His name. They must see God in me, and I must see God in them. Not to change the name of their religion, but to take their hand and say, "Come, let us look for God."

A few days ago as we came on the priests, they were praying, in one boat with thirty-five Moros, many of whom called to me to join. So I held out my hands and prayed with them, and as earnestly as any of them. One of them said, "He is Islam," and I replied, "A friend of Islam."

My teacher, Dato Pambaya, told me this week that a good Muslim ought to utter the sacred word for God every time he begins to do anything, to sleep, or walk, or work, or even turn around. A good Muslim would fill his life with God. I fear there are few good Muslims.

But so would a real Christlike Christian speak to God every time he did anything—and I fear there are few good Christians.

What right then have I or any other person to come here and change the name of these people from Muslim to Christian, unless I lead them to a life fuller of God than they have now? Clearly, clearly, my job here is not to go to the town plaza and make proselytes, it is to *live* wrapped in God, trembling to His thoughts, burning with His passion. And, my loved one, that is the best gift you can give to your own town.

I look up at this page and it is not red hot as my soul is now. It is black ink. It ought to be written with the red ribbon. You will not see the tears that are falling on this typewriter, tears of a boundless joy broken loose.

The most wonderful discovery that has ever come to me is that I do not have to wait until some future time for the glorious hour. I need not sing, "Oh that will be glory for me"—and wait for any grave. *This hour* can be heaven. *Any* hour for *any* body can be as rich as God! For do you not see that God is trying experiments with human lives. That is why there are so many of them. He has one billion seven hundred million experiments going on around the world at this moment. And His question is, "How far will this man and that woman allow me to carry this hour?" This Sunday afternoon at three o'clock He was asking it of us all. I do not know what the rest of you said, but as for me, I asked, "God, how wonderful dost Thou wish this hour alone with Thee to be?"

"It can be as wonderful as any hour that any human being has ever lived. For I who pushed life up through the protozoan and the tiny grass, and the fish and the bird and the dog and the gorilla and the man, and who am reaching out toward divine sons, I have not become satisfied yet. I am not only willing to make this hour marvelous. I am in travail to set you akindle with the Christ-thing which has no name. How fully can you surrender and not be afraid?"

And I answered: "Fill my mind with Thy mind to the last crevice. Catch me up in Thine arms and make this hour as terribly glorious as any human being ever lived, if Thou wilt.

"And God, I scarce see how one could live if his heart held more than mine has had from Thee this past two hours."

Will they last? Ah, that is the question I must not ask. I shall just live this hour on until it is full, then step into the next hour. Neither tomorrow matters, nor yesterday. Every now is an eternity if it is full of God.

But how "practical" is this for the average man? It seems to me now that yonder plowman could be like Calixto Sanidad, when he was a lonesome and mistreated plowboy, "with my eyes on the furrow, and my hands on the lines, but my thoughts on God." The carpenter could be as full of God as was Christ when he drove nails. The millions at looms and lathes could make the hours glorious. Some hour spent by some night watchman might be the most glorious ever lived on earth. God is not through yet. He is breaking through, and I think the poor have less callousness for Him to overcome as a rule than have the rich.

On the other hand, the rich man has the wonderful opportunity of paying a sacrifice which will cut his heart almost out. If he seeks the place where his wealth is needed most, then throws all he has into that cause and then throws himself into the cause with his money, as Jesus asked the rich young ruler to do, his money will at that moment be transmuted into the golden threads of heaven. Maybe there is another way, but to me there seems only a blank wall for wealthy men save through the doorway I have entered, a sacrifice that hurts and hurts and—behind Calvary, God!

Outside the sky is alight with golden sunset. To me that is God, working on the sky, as He has worked so wonderfully this afternoon within me.

15 MARCH 1930

DANSALAN • LAKE LANAO, PHILIPPINES

If these letters are to be given a name, I think it must be "The Story of a Reconversion," for something of this sort is still in progress. This week a new and to me marvelous experience has come out of my loneliness. I have been so desperately lonesome that it was unbearable save by talking with God. And so every waking moment of the week I have been looking toward Him, with perhaps the exception of an hour or two.

Last Thursday night I was listening to a phonograph in Lumbatan and allowing my heart to commune, when something broke within me, and I longed not only to lift my own will up and give it completely to God, but also to lift all the wills in the world up and offer them all in utter surrender to His will. To feel this great longing as I felt it then with all my being, to desire to put one's shoulder under all the world's hunger and need, and to carry it all to God, is not this the highest longing one can ever feel? Probably not, but it is the climax of my spiritual experience to this date.

God, be the thought within my brain, and be the thought in every brain in the world, so that no thought save the thoughts of God shall take birth in any human mind. And this will be heaven!

How infinitely richer this direct firsthand grasping of God Himself is than the old method which I used and recommended for years, the reading of endless devotional books. Almost it seems to me now that the very Bible cannot be read as a substitute for meeting God soul to soul and face to face. And yet, how was this new closeness achieved? Ah, I know now that it was by cutting the very heart of my heart and by suffering. Somebody was telling me this week that nobody can make a violin speak the last depths of human longing until that soul has been made tender by some great anguish. I do not say it is the only way to the heart of God, but I must witness that it has opened an inner shrine for me which I never entered before.

You and you and you and I *do* experience fine fresh contact with God sometimes, and do carry out His will sometimes. One question now to be put to the test is this: Can we have that contact with God all the time? All the time awake, fall asleep in His arms, and awaken in His presence, can we attain that? Can we do His will all the time? Can we think His thoughts all the time?

Or are there periods when business, and pleasures, and crowding companions must necessarily push God out of our thoughts? "Of course, that is self-evident. If one thinks of God all the time, he will never get anything else done." So I thought too, until now, but I am changing my view. We can keep two things in mind at once. Indeed we cannot keep one thing in mind more than half a second. Mind is a flowing something. It oscillates. Concentration is merely the continuous return to the same problem from a million angles. We do not think of one thing. We always think of the relationship of at least two things, and more often of three or more things simultaneously. So my problem is this: Can I bring God back in my mind-flow every few seconds so that God shall always be in my mind as an after image, shall always be one of the elements in every concept and percept?

I choose to make the rest of my life an experiment in answering this question.

Someone may be saying that this introspection and this struggle to achieve God-consciousness is abnormal and perilous. I am going to take the risks, for somebody ought to do it, in this day when psychological experimentation has given a fresh approach to our spiritual problems. If our religious premises are correct at all, then this oneness with God is the *most* normal condition one can have. It is what made Christ, Christ. It is what St. Augustine meant when he said, "Thou hast made us for Thyself, and our souls are restless until they find their rest in Thee."

I do not invite anybody else to follow this arduous path. I wish many might. We need to know so much which one man alone cannot answer. For example:

"Can a laboring man successfully attain this continuous surrender to God? Can a man working at a machine pray for people all day long, talk with God all day long, and at the same time do his task efficiently?"

"Can a merchant do business, can an accountant keep books, ceaselessly surrendered to God?"

"Can a mother wash dishes, care for the babies, continuously talking to God?"

"Can a politician keep in a state of continuous contact with God, and not lose the following of the crowds?"

"Can little children be taught to talk and listen to God inwardly all day long, and what is the effect upon them?"

Briefly, is this a thing which the entire human race might conceivably aspire to achieve? Do we really mean what we say when we repeat "the highest end of man is to find God and to do His will" all the time?

If you are like myself this has been pretty strong diet this afternoon. It may even prove discouraging. So I will put something simpler and more attainable:

"Any hour of any day may be made perfect by merely choosing. It is perfect if one looks toward God that entire hour, waiting for His leadership all through the hour and trying hard to do every tiny thing exactly as God wishes it done, as perfectly as possible. No emotions are necessary. Just the doing of God's will perfectly makes the hour a perfect one. And the results of that one perfect hour, I believe, will echo down through eternity."

DANSALAN • LAKE LANAO, PHILIPPINES

18 APRIL 1930

I have tasted a thrill in fellowship with God which has made anything discordant with God disgusting. This afternoon the possession of God has caught me up with such sheer joy that I thought I never had known anything like it. God was so close and so amazingly lovely that I felt like melting all over with a strange blissful contentment. Having had this experience, which comes to me now several times a week, the thrill of filth repels me, for I know its power to drag me from God. And after an hour of close friendship with God my soul feels as clean as new-fallen snow.

Everywhere people are beautiful—or at least they have a beautiful side. On the boat from Manila last week was a painted woman, alone. I spoke to her because she was lonesome. Three of the ship's officers nearby tittered as though they thought a scandal was brewing, so I talked loud enough for them to hear. I told her I was looking for God. As naturally as a preacher she replied, "God is everywhere around us and in us if we only open our eyes. *All the world is beautiful* if we have eyes to see the beauty, for the world is packed with God." "Thank you for that," I said, "I love it! What are you going to Cebu for?" "To put on my special act. You see I dance before seven mirrors. Nobody else in the world, so far as I know, has just this act. I am traveling alone, making my own engagements, for it is too expensive to have a property man. I was treated wonderfully well through India, *wonderfully* well!" I liked the way she pronounced that word, and the memories which lingered in her tired eyes. "And many people in Manila wrote me lovely letters, asking me to come back. Oh, the world is full of good people, full of good people." When the dinner bell rang I said, "I am going about the world trying to find wonderful hours, and I shall remember this as one of them."

This *conscious*, incessant submission to God has proven extremely difficult, and I have surrendered for the past few days. And today and yesterday I saw evidences of the result. In an effort to be witty, I have said biting things which have hurt the feelings of others, and have been short and impatient. I tremble, for I have told at least one of these men of this experiment, and he will think this is the result. It is very dangerous to tell people, and yet, I must tell and I *must* start over *now* and succeed. This philosophy that *one can begin all over instantly at any moment* is proving of great help.

If this record of a soul struggle to find God is to be complete, it must not omit the story of difficulty and failure. I have not succeeded very well so far. This week, for example, has not been one of the finest in my life, though it has been above the average. I have to make a greater effort next week. I have undertaken something which, at my age at least, is hard, harder than I had anticipated. But I resolve not to give up the effort.

Yet strain does not seem to do good. At this moment I feel something "let go" inside, and lo, God is here! It is a heart-melting "here-ness," a lovely whispering of father to child, and the reason I did not have it before was because I failed to let go.

And back of that failure there was something else. A crowd of people arrived who, when they are in a crowd, wish to talk or think nothing of religion. I fear I have not wanted some of them to think me religious for fear I might cease to be interesting.

Fellowship with God is something one dare not cover, for it smothers to death. It is like a tender infant or a delicate little plant, for a long nurturing is the price of having it, while it vanishes in a second of time, the very moment indeed one's eye ceases to be "single." One cannot worship God and Mammon for the reason that God slips out and is gone as soon as we try to seat some other unworthy affection beside Him. The other idol stays and God vanishes. Not because God is "a jealous God" but because sincerity and insincerity are contradictions and cannot both exist at the same time in the same place.

22 APRIL 1930

DANSALAN · LAKE LANAO · PHILIPPINES

The "experiment" is interesting, although I am not very successful, thus far. The idea of God slips out of my sight for I suppose two-thirds of every day, thus far. This morning I started out fresh, by finding a rich experience of God in the sunrise. Then I tried to let Him control my hands while I was shaving and dressing and eating breakfast. Now I am trying to let God control my hands as I pound the typewriter keys. If I could keep this morning up I should have a far higher average today than I have had for some time.

This afternoon as I look at the people teeming about me, and then think of God's point of view, I feel that this mighty stretch of time in which He has been pushing men upward is to continue for many more millions of years. We are yet to become what the spiritual giants have been and more than many of them were. Here the selection favors those who keep themselves wide open toward God and wide awake. Our possibilities are perhaps not limitless, but they are at least infinitely above our present possibilities of imagination.

There is nothing that we can do except to throw ourselves open to God. There is, there must be, so much more in Him than He can give us, because we are so sleepy and because our capacity is so pitifully small. It ought to be tremendously helpful to be able to acquire the habit of reaching out strongly after God's thoughts, and to ask, "God what have You to put into my mind now if only I can be large enough?" That waiting, eager attitude ought to give God the chance He needs. I am finding every day that the best of the five or six ways in which I try to keep contact with God is for me to *wait for His thoughts, to ask Him to speak.*

DANSALAN • LAKE LANAO, PHILIPPINES

14
MAY
1930

Oh, this thing of keeping in constant touch with God, of making Him the object of my thought and the companion of my conversations, is the most amazing thing I ever ran across. *It is working.* I cannot do it even half of a day—not yet, but I believe I shall be doing it some day for the entire day. It is a matter of acquiring a new habit of thought. Now I *like* God's presence so much that when for a half hour or so He slips out of mind—as He does many times a day—I feel as though I had deserted Him, and as though I had lost something very precious in my life.

This has been a week of wonders. God is at work *everywhere* preparing the way for His work in Lanao. I shall tell you some of the wonders presently. But just at this moment you must hear more of this sacred evening. The day had been rich but strenuous, so I climbed "Signal Hill," back of my house, talking and listening to God all the way up, all the way back, all the lovely half hour on the top. And God talked back! I let my tongue go loose and from it there flowed poetry far more beautiful than any I ever composed. It flowed without pausing and without ever a failing syllable for a half hour. I listened astonished and full of joy and gratitude. I wanted a Dictaphone for I knew that I should not be able to remember it—and now I cannot. "Why," someone may ask, "did God waste His poetry on you alone, when you could not carry it home?" You will have to ask God that question. I only know He did and I am happy in the memory.

Below me lay the rice fields and as I looked across them, I heard my tongue saying aloud, "Child, just as the rice needs the sunshine every day, and could not grow if it had sun only once a week or one hour a day, so you need me all day of every day. People over all the world are withering because they are open toward God only rarely. Every waking minute is not too much."

A few months ago I was trying to write a chapter on the "discovering of God." Now that I have discovered Him I find that it is a continuous discovery. Every day is rich with new aspects of Him and His working. As one makes new discoveries about his friends by being with them, so one discovers the "individuality" of God if one entertains Him continuously. One thing I have seen this week is that God loves beauty. Everything He makes is lovely. The clouds, the tumbling river, the waving lake, the soaring eagle, the slender blade of grass, the whispering of the wind, the fluttering butterfly, this graceful transparent nameless child of the lake which clings to my window for an hour and vanishes for ever. Beautiful craft of God! And I know that He makes my thought-life beautiful when I am open all the day to Him. If I throw these mind-windows apart and say "God, what shall we think of now?" He answers always in some graceful, tender dream. And I know that God is love-hungry, for He is constantly pointing me to some dull, dead soul which He has never reached and wistfully urges me to help Him reach that stolid, tight-shut mind. Oh God, how I long to help you with these Moros. And with these Americans! And with these Filipinos! All day I see souls dead to God look sadly out of hungry eyes. I want them to know my discovery! That any minute can be paradise, that any place can be heaven! That any man can have God! That every man *does have God* the moment he speaks to God, or listens for Him!

As I analyze myself I find several things happening to me as a result of these two months of strenuous effort to keep God in mind every minute. This concentration upon God is *strenuous*, but everything else has ceased to be so. I think more clearly, I forget less frequently. Things which I did with a strain before, I now do easily and with no effort whatever. I worry about nothing, and lose no sleep. I walk on air a good part of the time. Even the mirror reveals a new light in my eyes and face. I no longer feel in a hurry about anything. Everything goes right. Each minute I meet calmly as though it were not important. Nothing can go wrong except one thing. That is that God *may slip from my mind* if I do not keep on my guard. If He is there, the universe is with me. My task is simple and clear.

And I witness to the way in which the world reacts. Take Lanao and the Moros for illustration. Their responsiveness is to me a continuous source of amazement. I do nothing that I can see except to pray for them, and to walk among them thinking of God. They know I am a Protestant; yet two of the leading Moslem priests have gone around the province telling everybody that I would help the people to know God.

1
JUNE
1930

Inwardly this has been a very uneven week. As a whole, my end of the experiment has been failure for most of the week. My physical condition and too many distractions have proven too much for me, and God has not been in the center of my mind for one-fifth of the time, or perhaps one-tenth. But today has been a wonderful day, and some of yesterday was wonderful. The week with its failures and successes has taught me one new lesson. It is this: "I must talk about God, or I cannot keep Him in my mind. I must give Him away in order to have Him." That is the law of the spirit world. What one gives one has, what one keeps to oneself one loses.

Do you suppose that through all eternity the price we will need to pay for keeping God will be that we must endlessly be giving Him away?

This experiment which I am trying is the most strenuous discipline which any man ever attempted. I am not succeeding in keeping God in my mind very many hours of the day, and from the point of view of experiment number one, I should have to record a pretty high percentage of failure. But the other experiment—what happens when I do succeed—is so successful that it makes up for the failure of number one. God does work a change. The moment I turn to Him it is like turning on an electric current which I feel through my whole being. I find also that the effort to keep God in my mind does something to my mind which every mind needs to have done to it. I am given something difficult enough to keep my mind with a keen edge. The constant temptation of every man is to allow his mind to grow old and lose its edge. I feel that I am perhaps more lazy mentally than the average person, and I require the very mental discipline which this constant effort affords.

So my answer to my two questions to date would be

1. "Can it be done all the time?" Hardly.

2. "Does the effort help?" Tremendously. Nothing I have
   ever found proves such a tonic to mind and body.

Are you building sacred palaces for yourself? I meant to
write "places" to be sure, but I think I shall leave the word
"palaces," for that is what any house becomes when it is
sacred. The most important discovery of my whole life is
that one can take a little rough cabin and transform it into a
palace just by flooding it with thoughts of God. When one
has spent many months in a little house like this in daily
thoughts about God, the very entering of the house, the very
sight of it as one approaches, starts associations which set
the heart tingling and the mind flowing. I have come to the
point where I must have my house, in order to write the best
letters or think the richest thoughts.

So in this sense one man after the other builds his own
heaven or his hell. It does not matter where one is, one
can at once *begin to build heaven*, by thoughts which one
thinks while in that place... I have learned the secret of
heaven-building—anywhere.

This morning I read awhile about the tremendous consecration with which the scientists are studying the finest details about the sun, in an effort to find how to predict the weather, and to know how to use its power. And I feel that not yet have I thrown myself into the crucible of this experiment of mind with all the abandon of the successful scientist. We have heard the saying "All a man's failures are inside himself." And I am willing to confess that as yet I have not "striven unto blood" to win this battle. What I want to prove is that the thing *can be done* by all people under all conditions, but I have not proven it yet. This much I do see—what an incredibly high thing Jesus did.

A great lonesome hunger comes over me at this moment for someone who has passed through the same long, long channels of hope, and aspiration, and despair, and failure, to whom I can talk tonight. And yet—there is no such person. As we grow older all our paths diverge, and in all the world I suppose I could find nobody who could wholly understand me except God—and neither can you! Ah, God, what a new nearness this brings for Thee and me, to realize that Thou alone canst understand me, for Thou alone knowest all! Thou art no longer a stranger, God! Thou art the only being in the universe who is not partly a stranger! I invite others inside but they cannot come all the way. Thou art all the way inside with me—*here*—and every time I forget and push Thee out, Thou art eager to return! Ah, God, I mean to struggle tonight and tomorrow as never before, *not once* to dismiss Thee. For when I lose Thee for an hour, I lose and the world loses more than we can know. The thing Thou wouldst do can only be done when Thou hast full swing *all the time.*

I walk out in the street full of Moros, and if my soul is as full of God as it sometimes is, I see what happens as I look into their eyes and pray for them. No man need try to persuade me that God does not reach them, for I see the thing happen, and now I know that every person we ever meet is God's opportunity, if only, if only we were not so much of the time shut off from God.

Last Monday was the most completely successful day of my life to date so far as giving my day in complete and continuous surrender to God is concerned—though I shall hope for far better days—and I remember how as I looked at people with a love God gave, they looked back and acted as though they wanted to go with me. I felt then that for a day I saw a little of that marvelous pull that Jesus had as He walked along the road day after day, "God-intoxicated" and radiant with the endless communion of His soul with God.

DANSALAN · LAKE LANAO · PHILIPPINES

22 JUNE 1930

I have just returned from a walk alone, a walk so wonderful that I feel like reducing it to a universal rule, that all people ought to take a walk every evening all alone where they can talk aloud without being heard by anyone, and that during this entire walk they all ought to talk with God, allowing Him to use their tongue to talk back—and letting God do most of the talking.

For this seems to be the very thing for which I have been feeling all these weeks. You have followed my experiment and have seen many confessions of daily failure, as I tried to keep God in mind in the second person. Well, today has not been a failure. The thought of God has drifted out occasionally but not for long. But this day has been a different day from any other of my life, for I have not tried to pray in the sense of talking to God but I have let God do the talking with my tongue or in my inner life when my tongue was silent. It has been as simple as opening and closing a swinging door. And without any of the old strain, the whole day passed beautifully with God saying wonderful things to me.

The newest experiment, and at present the most thrilling, is letting God talk through my own tongue and through my own fingers on the typewriter. I have been letting my tongue talk on Signal Hill behind my house and then have come home and written on the typewriter all I could remember of it. Here is one sample: "I speak to you, not through your tongue only, but also through everything which you see in nature through the beauty of this sunset, through the little Moro boy who stands beside you without understanding what you are saying, and who wonders what you are looking at in the clouds. If I do not speak to you in words at times, it is because the reality all about you is greater than the imperfect symbols of things which you have in words. It is not necessary for your tongue to speak, nor even for any definite thoughts to light your mind, for I myself am infinitely more important for you than anything I can give you—even than the most brilliant thoughts. So when thoughts do come, welcome them, and when they do not flow freely, simply rest back and love, and grant me the shared joy of being loved by you. For I, too, by my very nature, am hungry with an insatiable hunger for the love of all of you, just as your love reaches out at your highest moments to all the people about you. So child, I, even I, God, whom people have foolishly feared and flattered for my gifts, I want love and friendship more than I want groveling subjects. So while we love each other, child, my share is as keen as yours."

I have written in this letter what my tongue said as I let it speak, not because I wish to recommend any of the above as prophetic, but simply because I think it may prove helpful to those who have been dissatisfied with their own contact with God and who may find this a helpful practice in making contacts with God. Day after day I find this very helpful in little intimate personal ways, which would have no value for others.

I am well aware of the probability of criticism because it is "mysticism"—as though any man could be a believer in Jesus without believing in "mysticism"!—or because many people think that the days of direct contact with God, or at least words from God, stopped with the closing of the New Testament. But then what a stupid world this would be if one never did anything different for fear of criticism!

Never did I so feel the need of a silent typewriter as at this moment, for every stroke clashes with the marvelous silence of the hills tonight. I am still under the spell of that hush and of that sunset. In all my life I have never seen a sight so beautiful as Lanao tonight … I suppose there have been equally beautiful scenes since the world was created, but not more beautiful for me. For it adequately reflected the passion of love which I feel toward the Lanao people as I look and pray from the hill.

And as I talked and tasted the sweetness of the luscious light, and told God that this was for me the masterpiece of His creation, he told me through my own voice: "Ah, child, this is but the symbol of beauties and wonders which I mean to give you when you are willing and ready. I must give them, I will give them, if only you will climb your spiritual hill and open your soul eyes and look. *This* is what all life can have if you are willing. I ache with longings which poor little people cannot even suspect, to open up wider and ever wider universes of glory to you all."

If asked my chief difficulty in meeting these Moros, I should have to reply, "No chief difficulty except to keep ready spiritually." And I wonder whether here is not the only serious difficulty anywhere. This year I am readier than I have ever been before, and perhaps this is why people seem readier also.

21 AUGUST 1930

I shall be forty-six in two weeks. I no longer have the sense that life is all before me, as I had a few years ago. Some of it is behind—and a miserable poor past it is, so far below what I had dreamed that I dare not even think of it. Nor dare I think much of the future. This present, if it is full of God, is the only refuge I have from poisonous disappointment and even almost rebellion against God. Here is this book of Reinhold Niebuhr, a man who seems to pour out wonderful thought as easily as one pours coffee. Why could not the rest of the world, including of course myself, be gifted like he is? And so many of the people here, and everywhere, seem to have more cramped lives and hopeless minds even than I have. I have been trying to teach a boy to read this afternoon, but his mind seems to be like pouring water into a mosquito net. He could not pronounce "i" without forgetting "a." What a tragedy to live in the world he lives in! I felt a warm love for the boy, and he felt it, for his eyes were moist as he told me he had neither father nor mother. At times when one looks out upon life all one sees are wrecks, and in upon life, too—wrecks! Ah, God, what is all this wreckage for?

I sat leaning upon my typewriter for a long while after that sentence, for a voice began to talk to me. "The wreckage is the birth pangs of love." And when I wanted to put my arm around that dirty, cross-eyed orphan Moro with his stupid brain, I was proving that ...

As I sit over in that old building day after day patiently toiling with one man or boy to teach him the alphabet, and so hold him to a larger world, I often wonder whether this work is becoming to a man of my age. But when that same man fondly runs his fingers through my hair and looks his love while he says "Mapia bapa"—good uncle—I know that a little love is created. If this entire universe is a desperate attempt of love to incarnate itself, then "important duties" which keep us from helping little people are not duties but sins—or am I all the while trying to justify my own failure?

Home from a wonderful hour with God in the sunset. Oh, those colors, those awful piles of clouds, those misty mysteries, those silent changes across the sky. If one could only forget oneself entirely and enjoy the universe—but some of us are too selfish to wipe ourselves out of the picture. We are deep-sea fish. They say there are fish under the ocean which are under such pressure that they dare not come near the surface or they perish. We are just that sort of fish, for we dare not venture far above the bottom of the atmosphere-ocean, or we die. We are not fish; we are worms on the bottom, for we cannot even swim in our ocean. And we are as little mentally as we are physically, and as tied to the bottom. Poor worms! And I suppose that this self-pity on this page is an excellent illustration of our littleness. When I feel like blaming God, then at that moment I show the real ugliness of my selfishness—for I know perfectly well that I should be quite complacent about all the innumerable creatures below man, and about all the innumerable creatures who are barely man, about the creatures who are robbed of their manhood by other selfish creatures like myself. I should not blame God for all these if I had all I wanted.

Here I was engaging in the most glorious action of all human and of all superhuman life—I was communing with the very God of the universe Himself. He was showing me His very heart; even the angels can do no more than this. I forgot that my being choked down against the bottom of an ocean like an octopus, and like an octopus in disposition, too, makes no difference at all. A prison or a dungeon makes no difference if one is with God. We preach and profess that as true, and it is true, but upon my word I do not see many people who seem to have experienced it. I am exactly like these Moro women and children. "Bapa," they say, "may I have this?" If I say "Yes," they forget to take it, but if I say "No," they beg me for it.

2 SEPTEMBER 1930

DANSALAN • LAKE LANAO • PHILIPPINES

Tip and I and God were together tonight on Signal Hill. Oh God, let me put on paper the glory that was there. The sunset was not more beautiful than at other times, but God said more in it. I suppose it was because I was trying to make this first day of my forty-sixth year high. And that I suppose is why all of us have some high days and some low ones. God is always awaiting the chance to give us high days. We so seldom are in deep earnest about giving Him His chance.

But the effort to say this colossal thing throws me into despair. It cannot be said, can it even be hinted at? There were black clouds which swiftly turned crimson and pale yellow. Now those black clouds are shooting out their fiery tongues through the darkness.

Far off in the middle of the lake, a long perfect waterspout stood like a colossal pillar from the clouds to the splashing water. It was the first perfect waterspout that I have seen from sea to sky. Above my head those black, angry clouds turned into glorious gold, from the hidden sun. But it was not this that made the evening wonderful. God was speaking.

I patted Tip's head as he nestled up under my arm, and told him: "We are two tiny insects in the midst of this terrifying universe. I know a little more than you do, you nice black dog, but not much more. Compared with the gigantic Being who wheels these awful spheres of fire through the sky, I am as near nothing as you are. I know as little about God as you know about me, perhaps ten thousand times less. And perhaps you are wiser than I, for you are contented to be patted on the head and to hunt for fleas, while I am impatient to break loose into the universe. I thought, Tip, when I was younger, that Kant was wrong when he said the three greatest moral demands are God, freedom, and immortality, but now I believe he was incredibly right. My soul at forty-six demands immortality as much as it demands God. And it demands freedom from this prison we call the world and the flesh as much as it demands immortality."

Then out of the skies there came a silent voice, "Your black clouds give the sun its chance. It is surprise, it is escape from darkness to light that makes life so rich. Your prison is also your paint box from which all the beauty you know is pouring. Lanao, where you now sit, is one of the most beautiful creations in all the reaches of space. And here you have the privilege of opening eyes to see beauty, which otherwise would not see. It is selfish of you to desire to escape, until you can take humanity with you. You are not Christlike until you demand that even after you die, your soul shall stay and help others come through to the larger life. I almost fear that my nightly visions, much as I love to give them to you, are making you more selfish, more hungry to get, less eager to give. The most beautiful thing in the universe for you is Lanao stretching around this lake at your feet, for it contains the beauty of immense need. You must awaken hunger there, for until they hunger they cannot be fed."

Oh, tonight I so hunger to be able to tell what else happened. But that other thing was all emotion, a painfully sweet stretching forth of arms skyward to receive and Lanaoward to give.

Our search for God through narrow straits has brought a sudden revelation, like an explorer who has just come out upon a limitless sea. It is not any particularly new idea but a new feeling, which came almost of itself. Today God seems to me to be just behind everything. I feel Him there. He is just under my hand, just under the typewriter, just behind this desk, just inside the file, just inside the camera.

One of these Moro fairy tales has the fairies standing behind every rock looking at the hero. That is how I feel about God today. Of course this is only a way of symbolizing the truth that God is invisible and that He is everywhere. I cannot imagine seeing the invisible, but I can imagine God hiding Himself behind everything in sight.

For a lonesome man there is something infinitely *homey* and comforting in feeling God so close, so *everywhere!* Nowhere one turns is away from friendship, for God is smiling there.

It is difficult to convey to another the *joy* of having broken into the new sea of realizing God's "here-ness." This morning our theme was "Jesus' view of prayer." It seemed so wonderfully true that just the privilege of fellowship with God is infinitely more than any *thing* that God could give. When He gives Himself He is giving more than anything else in the universe.

22 SEPTEMBER 1930

DANSALAN · LAKE LANAO, PHILIPPINES

We have got to saturate ourselves with the rainbows and the sunset marvels in order to radiate them. It is as much our duty to live in the beauty of the presence of God on some mount of transfiguration until we become white with Christ as it is for us to go down where they grope, and grovel, and groan, and lift them to new life. After all the deepest truth is that the Christlike life is glorious, undefeatably glorious. There is no defeat unless one loses God, and then all is defeat, though it be housed in castles and buried in fortunes.

It is that spirit of greed which Jesus said God hated more than any other. It is so diametrically opposite to the spirit of God. For God forever lavishes His gifts upon the good and bad alike, and finds all His joy in endless giving.

You see, I feel deeply about us all. Beside Jesus, the whole lot of us are so contemptible. I do not see how God stomachs us at all. But God is like Jesus, and He will not give up until we, too, are like Jesus.

**12
OCTOBER
1930**

How I wish, wish, wish that a dozen or more persons who are trying the experiment of holding God endlessly in mind would all write their experiences so that each would know what the other was finding as a result! The results, I think, would astound the world. At least the results of my own effort are astounding to me.

Worries have faded away like ugly clouds, and my soul rests in the sunshine of perpetual peace. I can lie down anywhere in this universe, bathed around by my own Father's Spirit. The very universe has come to seem so *homey*! I know only a little more about it than before, but that little is all! It is vibrant with the electric ecstasy of God! I know what it means to be "God-intoxicated."

How fine of these Moro boys to come and lean on one's knee, or run their fingers through one's hair—or rub the bald spots and ask why they are so! They know that we love them, but they do not realize what a gulf—at least historically—separates us. If they did, would they be so affectionate? If they knew *all*, if they knew the love of God in all its wondrous fervor, they would!

And to think that less than a year ago we were writing about "the most difficult place under the American flag, if not in the world!"

No, New York City is the most difficult place in the world, for in New York they demand ability, unusual ability, while here in Lanao, they demand only love—unusual love. And the love of God may be had for the receiving.

Has God ever struck you as the *Great Stirrer-Up*? One thing He seems to have determined is that we shall not fall asleep. We make or discover paradises for ourselves, and these paradises begin to lull us into sleepy satisfaction. Then God comes with His awakening hand, takes us by the shoulders, and gives us a thorough awakening.

And God knows we need it. If our destiny is to *grow* on and on and on, into some far more beautiful creatures than we are now, with more of the ideals of Christ, that means that we need to have the shells broken quite frequently so that we can grow.

My confidence that this earth is but a brief school grows into certainty as my fellowship with God grows more tender. As a discipline this world is admirable.

Jesus and Buddha had almost the same message about this life. Buddha said, "Abolish all desire." Jesus said, "Fix not your desires upon this earth, but lay up all the desires you can for a fuller life, which begins within you now, and is endless." Many people seek other escapes. Some in prodigious work, some in reckless play, some in drugs, some in insanity—for insanity is but an escape from pitiless, crushing failure. But I wish to tell all the world that needs a better way, that God on Signal Hill satisfies, and sends through me a glow of glory which makes me *sure* that this is the pathway of true intuition.

Sometimes one feels that there is a discord between the cross and beauty. But there really cannot be, for God is found best through those two doorways. This grey-blue rolling water tinged with whitecaps, hemmed with distant green hills, and crowned with colored clouds and baby-blue sky reveals God's love of beauty—and God is so lavish with His paintbrush in the tropics. He is lavish everywhere if one only has eyes to see Him at work.

But when one comes to personality, one demands more than a pretty face or even a soul that sings for joy. There is in the universe a higher kind of beauty. It is the beauty of sacrifice, of giving up for others, of suffering for others. A woman has not reached her highest beauty until she lays down her ease and chooses pain for bearing and nursing her child. A man has not found his highest beauty until his brow is tinged with care for some cause he loves more than himself. *The beauty of sacrifice is the final word in beauty.*

6
FEBRUARY
1931

DANSALAN • LAKE LANAO, PHILIPPINES

Tonight, lonesome and half ill with a cold, I am learning from experience that there is a deep peace that grows out of illness and loneliness and a sense of failure. These things do drive me up my hill to God, and then there comes into my soul through the very tears a comfort which is so much better than laughter. It is "the peace of God that passeth all understanding" unless one has it. God cannot get close when everything is delightful. He seems to need these darker hours, these empty-hearted hours to mean the most to people. You and I have known that over the coffin. We have known it when we parted and our hearts were sore. We have known it when we lay in bed helpless. Is this a deep truth in the very heart of nature? We sing,

> Nearer, my God, to Thee, nearer to Thee!
> E'en though it be a cross that raiseth me.

Is the cross the only doorway to the very heart of God?

10 FEBRUARY 1931

If there is any contribution that I have to make to the world that will live, surely it must be my experience of God on Signal Hill. This afternoon I climbed my way to the top, weighted with a sense of remorse. Everything wrong that I have done in twenty years came back and made me feel like a dreadful sinner. I told God about it, but do not intend to write any confessions here. We are so eager to judge people by their past, and it is not fair. We are what we are now, not an hour ago, and what we are planning, not what we are vainly trying to forget.

As I stood on the top, very much inclined to let the tears break out of my eyes, my tongue stopped talking to God and began talking from God to me: "Ah, little child, I have hurt you tonight, and now I feel sorry with you. All you have confessed is true, but I love you still. I love you for coming here and telling me about it. I love you for hungering after me. I love you for being willing to be better. That is all I ask of people. Ah, I have wanted to do so much for you as soon as you would allow it. Now, with a sore and lonesome heart you are ready. And after this torture, I must pull you close to my heart, tiny little one."

And into my heart, there stole another new love for God I never knew so strongly before. I felt like saying, "God, I do not know Thee nor this universe nor my own self. Everything becomes more mysterious the longer I think about it. But I thank Thee that Jesus showed us that Thou art burning, yearning, eager to do more for us than Thou canst. Thou art like those plowmen who must break the soil and tear it apart before seeds will grow. Thou hast plowed my heart tonight until it is tender and ready for something to grow. I thank Thee, God. I thank Thee because I could not have felt Thine healing hand if the pain had not been so acute.

"God, how can we reconcile this need of pain with our effort to abolish all misery?"

The answer seemed convincing to me: "If you abolish the physical suffering of the world, there will still be disappointed love, yearnings which cannot be satisfied, which will leave hearts bleeding even as they do today. Mansions have as many burning hearts as do poorhouses. The things which drag men down to grossness and incessant selfishness must be wiped out. Then hearts will become sore over infinitely larger things than selfish needs. They will learn to bleed for a world with the heart of Jesus." There will be more suffering than today, for only love knows how to suffer divinely. But the meanness of suffering for one's own selfish disappointments will be gone, and we will see a magnificence and sublimity in suffering that will make us glad.

As I lay on the warm earth on Signal Hill last night, I asked God the question, "Why is it that Thou dost allow us on this earth to do nearly all the talking? Why do we not always hear Thy voice, since Thou art so much wiser than we are?"

Instantly back came the answer. I could *see* it, from beginning to end in a second, though it may require more than a minute to write it down. So many of these thoughts from God are hurled at me in an instant like that: "When you are teaching the Moros to read, your art is to say as little as you can and leave them to say as much as they will. That is why I leave you to do and say as much as you can, while I say little. You learn by doing, even when you make mistakes and correct them. You are to be sons and daughters of God, and now you are taking the first feeble steps of an infant. Every step you take alone is infinitely more important than you now imagine, because the thing I am preparing you for exceeds all your imagination. So the talking you do to me is essential. The talking others do to you, when they are trying to talk up to your expectations, is more important than the talks you give to them. This is the best way to act: Talk a great deal to me. Let others talk a great deal to you, appreciating everything fine they say and neglecting their mistakes."

Oh, if we *only* let God have His *full* chance He will break our hearts with the glory of His revelation. That is the privilege which the preacher *can* have above others. It is his business to look into the very face of God until he aches with bliss. And that is how I feel this morning after two hours of wonderful thinking with God. And now on this "mount of transfiguration" I do not want ever to leave. I want to keep this lovely aching heart forever. But that would not be Christlike. I must now carry all I can of Him across the river to the Moro school. There are figures and there are salaries to be considered, for it is the end of the month. How much of this glory can one carry into business?

DANSALAN · LAKE LANAO · PHILIPPINES

5 APRIL 1931

We see ourselves on trial with Jesus. He could walk into the jaws of death to do His blessed work for others. He could dare to speak out against wrong and take the consequences. He could receive floggings, could allow men to spit in His face, could endure the agony of thorns in His head, could be taunted without a word or even a thought of anger, could think of His mother while writhing on the cross, could cry, "Father, forgive them, for they know not what they do." I have read books which said that these words were evidently imaginary for nobody *could* say anything when suffering the excruciating torture of hanging by nails. But Jesus was such an "impossible" person more than once in His life. This scene fits into His whole character. True, nobody else can think of others when suffering like that, but Jesus was better than the rest of us. Tragedy, magnificent horror! The best man who ever lived dying because He was too good to run away.

That would have driven humanity more deeply into despair. They might or might not have remembered Jesus. I think they would have tried to forget Him. For humanity wants to believe that God is good, and the crucifixion portrays God forsaking the finest example of loyalty we can find. God was betraying His staunchest defender. That cross alone is horrible. The God who would allow the drama to stop there would be a monster or dead. "My God, why...?"

So we cannot believe in a good God unless we have Easter. It is a difficult story to believe, because we have had nothing else quite like it before or since. But it is only the difficulty of believing the unprecedented. On the other hand to doubt it is far more difficult. I must either rule out the whole story of the life of Jesus or else rule out any intelligence or heart from the universe. And if I do that my troubles are far more than intellectual—they become moral. I cannot actually sacrifice myself for others, at least not to death, for, noble as it may sound, it is folly. The act of Jesus becomes not only rash and useless but misleading to the rest of mankind.

How it is proved? It isn't proved, you fool! It can't be proved. How can you prove a victory before it's won?

How can you prove a man who leads to be a leader worth following unless you follow to the death, and out beyond mere death, which is not anything but Satan's lie upon eternal life.... And you? You want to argue. Well, I won't. It's a choice, and I choose Christ.

—Studdert Kennedy

That last sentence is the crux of the whole matter; it is a choice, and while choosing Christ brings mystery, rejecting Him brings despair.

DANSALAN · LAKE LANAO. PHILIPPINES

28
SEPTEMBER
1931

The fashion today is to place God in court and give Him a trial. We have had such a lust for "debunking" every good and useful man in history that even God cannot escape. It is one of the unfortunate by-products of the quest for truth, plus an unlovely hunger in humanity for scandal. It is a species of jealousy. We dislike to believe that anybody else is quite as good as we are, not even God.

As for me, I choose to stop following this current, to stop posing as the judge of the universe. If it brought any good results I might continue, but to date it has carried me out into the desert and left me there. The books one reads also end on the desert.

I choose another road for myself. I choose to look at people through God, using God as my glasses, colored with His love for them.

Last year, as you know, I decided to *try* to keep God in mind all the time. That was rather easy for a lonesome man in a strange land. It has always been easier for the shepherds, and the monks, and anchorites than for people surrounded by crowds.

But today it is an altogether different thing. I am no longer lonesome. The hours of the day from dawn to bedtime are spent in the presence of others. Either this new situation will crowd God out or I must take Him into it all. I must learn a continuous silent conversation of heart to heart with God while looking into other eyes and listening to other voices. If I decide to do this it is far more difficult than the thing I was doing before.

Yet if this experiment is to have any value for busy people it must be worked under exactly these conditions of high pressure and throngs of people.

There is only one way to do it. God must share my thoughts of Moro grammar, and Moro epics, and type, and teaching people to read, and talking over the latest excitement with my family as we read the newspapers. So I am resolved to let nothing, *nothing*, stop me from this effort save sheer fatigue that stops all thought.

One need not tell God *everything* about the people for whom one prays. Holding them one by one steadily before the mind and willing that God may have His will with them is the best, for God knows better than we what our friends need, yet our prayer releases His power, we know not how….

This afternoon has brought a wonderful experience, all inside my own mind. I closed my eyes to pray and the faces of those before me, then those in the houses nearby, then those down the line, and across the river, and down the highway to the next town, and the next, and the next, then in concentric circles around the lake, and over the mountains to the coast, then across the sea to the north, then over the wide ocean to California, then across America to the people whom I know, then over to Europe to the people whom I have met there, then to the Near East where my missionary friends live, then to India where I have other friends, to others in China, and to the multitudes who are suffering the dreadful pangs of cold and starvation—around the world in less than a minute, and for a time the whole of my soul seemed to be lit up with a divine light as it held the world up to God!

I cannot get God by holding Him off at arm's length like a photograph, but by leaning forward intently as one would respond to one's lover. Love so insatiable as the love of God can never be satisfied until we respond to the limit. Nor will He be satisfied until His aching arms receive my neighbors, too, and all the surging multitudes of the world, all of us together responding to Him and to one another.

When one has struck some wonderful blessing that all mankind has a right to know about, no custom or false modesty should prevent him from telling it, even though it may mean the unbarring of his soul to the public gaze.

I have found such a way of life. I ask nobody else to live it, or even to try it. I only witness that it is wonderful, it is indeed heaven on earth. And it is very simple, so simple that any child could practice it. Just to pray inwardly for everybody one meets, and to keep on all day without stopping, even when doing other work of every kind.

This simple practice requires only a gentle pressure of the will, not more than a person can exert easily. It grows easier as the habit becomes fixed.

Yet it transforms life into heaven. Everybody takes on a new richness, and all the world seems tinted with glory. I do not of course know what others think of me, but the joy which I have within cannot be described. If there never were

any other reward than that, it would more than justify the
practice to me.

Today I have noticed that when I forget other people I
become fatigued rather quickly. When I am reminded of my
purpose and start again holding people, seen and unseen,
before God, a new exhilaration comes to me, and all the
fatigue vanishes.

11 OCTOBER 1931

DANSALAN • LAKE LAMAO, PHILIPPINES

Knowing God better and better is an achievement of friendship. "When two persons fall in love there may be such a strong feeling of fellowship, such a delight in the friend's presence, that one may lose oneself in the deepening discovery of another person." The self and the person loved become equally real.

There are, therefore, three questions which we may ask: "Do you believe in God?" That is not getting very far. "The devils believe and tremble." Second, "Are you acquainted with God?" We are acquainted with people with whom we have had some business dealings. Third, "Is God your friend?" or putting this another way, "Do you love God?"

It is this third stage that is really vital. How is it to be achieved? Precisely as any friendship is achieved—by doing things together. The depth and intensity of the friendship will depend upon variety and extent of the things we do and enjoy together. Will the friendship be constant? That again depends upon the permanence of our common interests, and upon whether or not our interests grow into ever-widening circles, so that we do not stagnate. The highest friendship demands growth. "It must be progressive as life itself is progressive." Friends must walk together; they cannot long stand still together, for that means death to friendship and to life.

Friendship with God is the friendship of child with parent. As an ideal son grows daily into closer relationship with his father, so we may grow into closer love with God by widening into His interests, and thinking His thoughts and sharing His enterprises.

Far more than any other device of God to create love was the cross where the *lovingest* person the world has known hangs loving through all His pain. That cross has become the symbol of religion and of love for a third of the world because it touches the deepest depths of human love.

All I have said is mere words, until one sets out helping God right wrongs, helping God help the helpless, loving and talking it over with God. Then there comes a great sense of the close-up, warm, intimate heart of reality. God simply creeps in and you *know* He is here in your heart. He has become your friend by working along with you.

So if anybody were to ask me how to find God I should say at once, hunt out the deepest need you can find and forget all about your own comfort while you try to meet that need. Talk to God about it, and—He will be there. You will know it.

In school a teacher lays out work for his pupils. I resolve to accept each situation of this year as God's layout for that hour, and never to lament that it is a very commonplace or disappointing task. One can pour something divine into every situation.

One of the mental characteristics against which I have rebelled most is the frequency of my "blank spells" when I cannot think of anything worth writing, and sometimes cannot remember names. Henceforth I resolve to regard these as God's signal that I am to stop and listen. Sometimes you want to talk to your son, and sometimes you want to hold him tight in silence. God is that way with us; He wants to hold still with us in silence.

Here is something we can share with all of the people in the world: They cannot all be brilliant or rich or beautiful. They cannot all even dream beautiful dreams like God gives some of us. They cannot all enjoy music. Their hearts do not all burn with love. But everybody can learn to hold God by the hand and rest. And when God is ready to speak, the fresh thoughts of heaven will flow in like a crystal spring. Everybody rests at the end of the day; what a world gain if everybody could rest in the waiting arms of the Father, and listen until He whispers.

PUBLISHER'S NOTE

Although *The Game with Minutes* was written in an earlier era, we encourage the reader to seek to grasp the concepts presented and not be distracted by particular examples or illustrations that reflect the times in which the author penned them.

The
GAME
with Minutes

PHILIPPINES

24
HOURS
A DAY

DANSALAN · LAKE LANAO

The GAME with Minutes

Frank C. Laubach

"Disillusioned by all our other efforts, we now see that the only hope left for the human race is to become like Christ." That is the statement of a famous scientist, and is being repeated among ever more educators, statesmen, and philosophers. Yet Christ has not saved the world from its present terrifying dilemma. The reason is obvious: few people are getting enough of Christ to save either themselves or the world. Take the United States, for example. Only a third of the population belongs to a Christian church. Less than half of this third attend service regularly. Preachers speak about Christ in perhaps one service in four—thirty minutes a month! Good sermons, many of them excellent, but too infrequent in presenting Christ.

Less than ten minutes a week given to thinking about Christ by one-sixth of the people is not saving our country or our world; for selfishness, greed, and hate are getting a thousand times that much thought. What a nation thinks about, that it is. We shall not become like Christ until we give Him more time. A teachers' college requires students to attend classes for twenty-five hours a week for three years. Could it prepare competent teachers or a law school prepare competent lawyers if they studied only ten minutes a week? Neither can Christ, and He never pretended that He could. To His disciples He said: "Come with me, walk with me, talk and listen to me, work and rest with me, eat and sleep with me, twenty-four hours a day for three years." That was their college course—"He chose them," the Bible says, "that they might be with Him," 168 hours a week!

All who have tried that kind of abiding for a month know the power of it—it is like being born again from center to circumference. It absolutely changes every person who does it. And it will change the world that does it.

How can a man or woman take this course with Christ today? The answer is so simple a child can understand it. Indeed unless we "turn and become like children" we shall not succeed.

1. We have a study hour. We read and reread the life of Jesus recorded in the Gospels thoughtfully and prayerfully at least an hour a day. We find fresh ways and new translations, so that this reading will never be dull, but always stimulating and inspiring. Thus we walk with Jesus through Galilee by walking with Him through the pages of His earthly history.

2. We make Him our inseparable chum. We try to call Him to mind at least one second of each minute. We do not need to forget other things nor stop our work, but we invite Him to share everything we do or say or think. Hundreds of people have experimented until they have found ways to let Him share every minute that they are awake. In fact, it is no harder to learn this new habit than to learn the touch system in typing, and in time one can win a high percentage of his minutes with as little effort as an expert needs to write a letter.

While these two practices take all our time, yet they do not take it away from any good enterprise. They take Christ into that enterprise and make it more resultful. They also keep a man's religion steady. If the temperature of a sick man rises and falls daily the doctor regards him as seriously ill. This is the case with religion. Not spiritual chills and fevers, but an abiding faith which gently presses the will toward Christ all day, is a sign of a healthy religion.

Practicing the presence of God is not on trial. It has already been proven by countless thousands of people. Indeed, the spiritual giants of all ages have known it. Christians who do it today become more fervent and beautiful and are tireless witnesses. Men and women who had been slaves of vices have been set free. Catholics and Protestants find this practicing the presence of God at the heart of their faith. Conservatives and liberals agree that here is a reality they need. People who are grateful for what this booklet has done for them are ordering wholesale quantities to give to friends. Letters from all parts of the world testify that in this game, multitudes are turning defeat into victory and despair into joy.

The results of this program begin to show clearly in a month. They grow rich after six months, and glorious after ten years.

Somebody may be saying, "All this is very orthodox and very ancient." It is, indeed, the secret of the great saints of all ages. "Pray without ceasing," said Paul. "In everything make your wants known unto God." "As many as are *led* by the Spirit of God these are the sons of God."

How We Win the Game with Minutes

Nobody is wholly satisfied with himself. Our lives are made up of lights and shadows, of some good days and many unsatisfactory days. We have learned that the good days and hours come when we are very close to Christ, and that the poor days come whenever we push Him out of our thoughts. Clearly, then, the way to a more consistent high level is to take Him into everything we do or say or think.

Experience has told us that good resolutions are not enough. We need to discipline our lives to an ordered regime. The "Game with Minutes" is a rather lighthearted name for such a regime in the realm of the spirit. Many of us have found it to be enormously helpful. It is a new name for something as old as Enoch, who "walked with God." It is a way of living which nearly everybody knows and nearly everybody has ignored. Students will at once recognize it as a fresh approach to Brother Lawrence's "Practicing the Presence of God."

We call this a "game" because it is a delightful experience and an exhilarating spiritual exercise; but we soon discover that it is far more than a game. Perhaps a better name for it would be "an exploratory expedition," because it opens out into what seems at first like a beautiful garden; then the garden widens into a country; and at last we realize that we are exploring a new world. This may sound like poetry, but it is not overstating what experience has shown us. Some people have compared it to getting out of a dark prison and beginning to LIVE. We still see the same world, yet it is not the same, for it has a new glorious color and a far deeper meaning. Thank God, this adventure is free for everybody, rich or poor, wise or ignorant, famous or unknown, with a good past or a bad—"Whosoever will, may come." The greatest thing in the world is for everybody!

You will find this just as easy and just as hard as forming any other habit. You have hitherto thought of God for only a few seconds or minutes a week, and He was out of your mind the rest of the time. Now you are attempting, like Brother Lawrence, to have God in mind each minute you are awake. Such drastic change in habit requires a real effort at the beginning.

Many of us find it very useful to have pictures of Christ where our eyes will fall on them every time we look around. A very happy hobby is to collect the most friendly pictures of Christ, pocket size, so that we can erect our own "shrine" in a few seconds.

How to Begin

Select a favorable hour; try how many minutes of the hour you can remember God at least ONCE each minute; that is to say, bring God to mind at least one second out of every sixty. It is not necessary to remember God *every second*, for the mind runs along like a rapid stream from one idea to another.

Your score will be low at first, but keep trying, for it constantly becomes easier, and after a while is almost automatic. It follows the well-known laws of habit forming. If you try to write shorthand you are at first very awkward. This is true when you are learning to play a piano, or to ride a bicycle, or to use any new muscles. When you try this "game with minutes" you discover that spiritually you are still a very weak infant. A babe in the crib seizes upon everything at hand to pull himself to his feet, wobbles for a few seconds and falls exhausted. Then he tries again, each time standing a little longer than before. We are like that babe when we begin to try to keep God in mind. We need something to which we can cling. Our minds wobble and fall, then rise for a new effort. Each time we try we shall do better until at last we may be able to remember God as high as 90 percent of the whole day.

How to Try the Experiment in Church

You have a good chance of starting well if you begin in church—provided the sermon is about God. When our congregation first tried it, we distributed slips of paper which read

Game with Minutes Scorecard

During this hour I thought of God at least

once each minute for _____ different minutes.

Signed   _____

At the opening of the service the pastor made this announcement: "Everybody will be asked to fill this scorecard at the end of one hour. In order to succeed, you may use any help within reach. You may look at the cross, or you may leaf through your hymnbook or Bible, looking for verses that remind you of God."

The sermon that Sunday explained how to play the game. At the end of the hour, the scorecards were collected. The congregation reported scores ranging from five to sixty minutes. The average was forty-four minutes, which meant 73 percent of the hour. For beginners this was excellent. Such an experiment, by the way, will encourage the congregation to listen better than usual, and will remind the preacher to keep his sermon close to God.

If you score 75 percent in church, you can probably make a rather good score for the rest of the day. It is a question of being master of every new situation.

Never use a scorecard more than an hour, and not that long if it tires you. This is a new delight you are learning, and it must not be turned into a task.

While Going Home from Church

Can you win your game with minutes while passing people on the street? Yes! Experiments have revealed a sure way to succeed: offer a swift prayer for the people at whom you glance. It is easy to think an instantaneous prayer while looking people straight in the eye, and the way people smile back at you shows that they like it! This practice gives a surprising exhilaration, as you may prove for yourself. A half-hour spent walking and praying for all one meets, instead of tiring one, gives him a sense of ever heightening energy like a battery being charged. It is a tonic, a good way to overcome a tired feeling.

Some of us walk on the right side of the pavement, leaving room for our unseen Friend, whom we visualize walking by our side, and we engage in silent conversations with Him about the people we meet. For example, we may say: "Dear Companion, what can we do together for this man whom we are passing?" Then we whisper what we believe Christ would answer.

WHERE TO LOOK FOR CHRIST

We have a right to use any aid that proves useful. One such aid is to think of Christ as in a definite location. To be sure, He is a spirit, everywhere at once—and therefore anywhere we realize Him to be. Many of us win our game nearly all of some days by realizing His unseen presence sitting in a chair or walking beside us. Some of us have gazed at our favorite picture of Him until it floats before our memories whenever we glance at His unseen presence, and we almost see Him. Indeed, many of us do see Him in our dreams. Others, like St. Paul, like to feel Him within the breast; many, like St. Patrick, feel Him all around us, above, below, before, behind, as though we walked in His kindly halo. We may have our secret ways of helping us to realize that He is very near and very dear.

On a Train or in a Crowd

We whisper "God" or "Jesus" or "Christ" constantly as we glance at every person near us. We try to see *double*, as Christ does—we see the person as he is and the person Christ longs to make him. Remarkable things happen, until those in tune look around as though you spoke—especially children. The atmosphere of a room changes when a few people keep whispering to Him about all the rest. Perhaps there is no finer ministry than just to be in meetings or crowds, whispering "Jesus," and then helping people whenever you see an opportunity. When Dr. Chalmers answers the telephone he whispers: "A child of God will now speak to me." We can do that when anybody speaks to us.

If everybody in America would do the things just described above, we should have a "heaven below." This is not pious poetry. We have *seen* what happens. Try it during all this week, until a strange power develops within you. As messages from England are broadcast in Long Island for all America, so we can become spiritual broadcasters for Christ. Every cell in our brain is an electric battery which He can use to intensify what He longs to say to people who are spiritually deaf to hear Him without our help.

While in Conversation

Suppose when you reach home you find a group of friends engaged in ordinary conversation. Can you remember God at least once every minute? This is hard, but we have found that we can be successful if we employ some reminders. Here are aids which have proven useful:

1. Have a *picture* of Christ in front of you where you can glance at it frequently.

2. Have an *empty chair* beside you and imagine that your Unseen Master is sitting in it; if possible reach your hand and touch that chair, as though holding His hand. He is there, for He said: "Lo, I am with you always."

3. Keep humming to yourself a favorite prayer *hymn*—for example, "Have Thine Own Way, Lord, Have Thine Own Way."

4. Silently *pray* for each person in the circle.

5. Keep *whispering* inside: "Lord, put Thy thoughts in my mind. Tell me what to say."

6. Best of all, tell your companions about the "Game with Minutes." If they are interested, you will have no more trouble. *You cannot keep God unless you give Him to others.*

WHEN AT THE TABLE

All the previous suggestions are useful at mealtime. If possible, have an empty chair for your Invisible Guest, who said, "Wherever two or three are gathered together, I am in the midst." Another useful aid is to recall what the Quakers believe about every meal. Jesus told us: "Eat this in remembrance of me." They think that He meant, not only consecrated bread, but all food so that every mouthful is His "body broken for you."

You might read and discuss this booklet. It helps immediately if others at the table agree to try to win this mealtime together.

WHILE READING A BOOK

When we are reading a newspaper or magazine or book, we read it to Him! We often glance at the empty chair where we visualize Him, or at His picture and continue a running conversation with Him inwardly about the pages we are reading. Kagawa says scientific books are letters from God telling how He runs His universe.

Have you ever opened a letter and read it *with* Jesus, realizing that He smiles with us at the fun, rejoices with us in the successes, and weeps with us at life's tragedies? If not, you have missed one of life's sweetest experiences.

When Thinking

If you lean back and think about some problem deeply, how can you remember God? You can do it by forming a new habit. All thought employs silent words and is really conversation with your inner self. Instead of talking to yourself, you will now form the habit of talking to Christ. Many of us who have tried this have found that we think so much better that we never want to try to think without Him again. We are helped if we imagine Him sitting in a chair beside us, talking with us. We say with our tongue what we think Christ might say in reply to our questions. Thus we *consult* Christ about everything.

WHEN WALKING ALONE

If you are strolling out of doors alone, you can recall God at least once every minute with no effort, if you remember that "beauty is the voice of God." Every flower and tree, river and lake, mountain and sunset, is God speaking. "This is my Father's world, and to my listening ears all nature sings …" So as you look at each lovely thing, you may keep asking: "Dear Father, what are you telling me through this, and this, and this?"

If you have wandered to a place where you can talk aloud without being overheard, you may speak to the Invisible Companion inside you or beside you. Ask Him what is most on His heart and then answer back aloud with your voice what you believe God would reply to you.

Of course we are not always sure whether we have guessed God's answer right, but it is surprising how much of the time we are very certain. It really is not necessary to be sure that our answer is right, for the answer is not the great thing—He is! God is infinitely more important than His advice or His gifts; indeed, *He, Himself, is the great gift.* The youth in love does not so much prize what his sweetheart may say or may give him, as the fact that she is *his* and that she is *here.* The most precious privilege in talking with God is this intimacy which we can have with Him. We may have a glorious succession of heavenly minutes. How foolish people are to lose life's most poignant joy, seeing it may be had while taking a walk alone!

But the most wonderful discovery of all is, to use the words of St. Paul, "Christ liveth in me." He dwells in us, walks in our minds, reaches out through our hands, speaks with our voices, IF we obey His every whisper.

BE MY LAST THOUGHT

We make sure that there is a picture of Christ, or a Bible, or a cross or some other object where it will greet our closing eyes as we fall asleep. We continue to whisper any words of endearment our hearts suggest. If all day long we have been walking with Him, we shall find Him the dear companion of our dreams. Sometimes after such a day, we have fallen asleep with our pillows wet from tears of joy, feeling His tender touch on our foreheads. Usually we feel no deep emotion, but always we have a "peace that passeth all understanding." This is the end of a perfect day.

MONDAY MORNING

If on Sunday we have rated over 50 percent in our game with minutes, we shall be eager to try the experiment during a busy Monday. As we open our eyes and see a picture of Christ on the wall, we may ask: "Now, Master, shall we get up?" Some of us whisper to Him our every thought about washing and dressing in the morning, about brushing our shoes and choosing our clothes. Christ is interested in every trifle, because He loves us more intimately than a mother loves her babe, or a lover his sweetheart, and is happy only when we share every question with Him.

MEN AT WORK

Countless thousands of men keep God in mind while engaged in all types of work, mental or manual, and find that they are happier and get better results. Those who endure the most intolerable ordeals gain new strength when they realize that their Unseen Comrade is by their side. To be sure, no man whose business is harmful or whose methods are dishonest can expect God's partnership. But if an enterprise is useful, God eagerly shares in its real progress. The carpenter can do better work if he talks quietly to God about each task, as

Jesus certainly did when He was a carpenter. Many of us have found that we can compose a letter or write a book better when we say "God, think Thy thoughts in my mind. What dost Thou desire written? Here is my hand; use it. Pour Thy wisdom through my hand." Our thoughts flow faster, and what we write is better. God loves to be a coauthor!

MERCHANTS AND BANKERS

A merchant who waits on his customers and prays for them at the same time wins their affection and their business. A salesman who prays for those with whom he is dealing has far more likelihood of making a sale. A bookkeeper or banker can whisper to God about every column of figures and be certain that God is even more interested in the figures than he is. The famous astronomer, Sir James Jeans, calls God the "super-mathematician of the universe, making constant use of mathematical formulae that would drive Einstein mad."

IN THE HOME

Many women cultivate Christ's companionship while cooking, washing dishes, sweeping, sewing, and caring for children. Aids which they find helpful are …

1. Whispering to God about each small matter, knowing that He loves to help.

2. Humming or singing a favorite prayer hymn.

3. Showing the children how to play the game with minutes, and asking them to share in playing it. Children love this game and develop an inner control when they play it which renders discipline almost needless.

4. Having pictures of Christ about the house, as a constant reminder.

5. Saying to God, "Think Thy thoughts in my mind."

WHEN IN SCHOOL

An increasing army of students in school who are winning this game, tell us how they do it. Here is their secret:

When in study period, say: "God, I have just forty precious minutes. Help my wavering thoughts to concentrate so that I may not waste a moment. Show me what is worth remembering in this first paragraph"—then read the lesson to God, instead of reading it to yourself.

When going to recitation, whisper: "Make my mind clear, so that I will be able to recall all I have studied. Take away fear."

When rising to recite before a group, say: "God, speak through my lips."

When taking an examination, say all during the hour, "Father, keep my mind clear, and help me to remember all that I have learned. How shall we answer this next question?" Visualize Him looking over your shoulder every minute you are writing. God will not tell you what you have never studied but He does sharpen your memory and take away your stage fright when you ask Him. Have you not discovered that when you pray about some forgotten name it often flashes into your memory?

To be sure, this prevents us from being dishonest or cheating, for if we are not honest we cannot expect His help. But this is a good reason for playing the game with minutes. Character is a hundred times more valuable than knowledge or high grades.

To be popular with the other students, acquire the habit of breathing a momentary prayer for each student you meet, and while you are in conversation with him. Some instinct tells him you are interested in his welfare and he likes you for it.

PRAYING HORSESHOES

A very powerful way to pray is for a group of friends to join hands while seated in the shape of a horseshoe. Some of us have an altar at the open end of the horseshoe, with a cross or a picture of Jesus, or a Bible, or a globe of the world. The horseshoe opens toward the cities, countries, and people most in need of prayer.

This horseshoe of prayer reminds us of the great magnets which can lift a locomotive when the electric power is turned on. We are seeking to be used by the inpouring Holy Spirit to lift the world, and to draw all men to Christ.

It also reminds us of the radio broadcast which, when the power is on, leaps around the world. We offer ourselves as God's broadcasting station.

The gentle tingle which we usually feel reminds us of the glow and soft purr in the tubes of a radio when the power is on.

Every Christian family at mealtime may form a prayer radio broadcast by joining hands. Young people's societies will love it. It will vitalize every Sunday school class to spend ten minutes in broadcasting. Defunct prayer meetings will come to life when they become horseshoe magnets of prayer.

Schools and colleges, public or private, will find prayer horseshoes popular with the students. Here is something that Christians and Jews can do together. Worship can thus be made the most thrilling experience of their lives.

The group may prepare a list of the most urgent world needs and of key persons. An excellent plan at breakfast is for someone to read from the newspaper the problems and persons which are most in need of prayer that morning.

The leader may say words like these: "Lord, in this terribly critical hour we want to do everything we can. We pray Thee, use us to help the President to be hungry for Thee, to listen and hear and obey Thee. We lift President Eisenhower into Thy presence."

Then all may raise their clasped hands toward heaven. And so with the entire list.

After the prayer list is completed, the globe of the world may be lifted toward God while somebody prays the Lord's Prayer.

DURING PLAY HOURS

God is interested in our fun as much as we are. Many of us talk to Him during our games. Some of the famous football players long ago discovered that they played better if they prayed all during the game. Some of the famous runners pray during races. If a thing brings health and joy and friendship and a fresh mind, God is keenly interested, because He is interested in us.

While on the playground, do not ask to win, but whisper: "God, get Thy will done exactly. Help us all to do our best. Give us what is far more important than defeating our opponents—make us clean sportsmen and make us good friends."

GOD AND LOVE

Sweethearts who have been wise enough to share their love with God have found it incomparably more wonderful. Since "God is Love" He is in deepest sympathy with every fond whisper and look. Husbands and wives, too, give rapturous testimony of homes transformed by praying silently when together. In some cases where they had begun to give each other "nerves," they have found, after playing this game when they are alone together by day or by night, that their love grew strangely fresh, rich, beautiful, "Like a new honeymoon." God is the maker of all true marriages, and He gives His highest joy to a man and wife who share their love for each other with Him, who pray inwardly each for the other when they are together looking into one another's eyes. Married love becomes infinitely more wonderful when Christ is the bond every minute and it grows sweeter as the years go by to the very last day. Imagine, too, what this does for the children!

TROUBLES

Troubles and pain come to those who practice God's presence, as they came to Jesus, but these seem trivial as compared to their new joyous experience. If we have spent our days with Him, we find that when earthquakes, fires, famines, or other catastrophes threaten us, we are not terrified any more than Paul was in time of shipwreck. "Perfect love casteth out Fear."

This booklet on the Game with Minutes is good for people suffering from illness at home or in hospitals. Nurses remind us that the thoughts of people turn toward God when sick as at no other time. Patients who are convalescing have many idle hours when their minds reach up toward God. Playing this game produces a perfect mental state for rapid recovery.

Those who are seeking to be aware of God constantly have found that their former horror at death has vanished. We may have a new mystic intimacy with our departed loved ones, for though unseen to us, they are with Christ and since He is with us they are with us as well.

SOME PRICES WE MUST PAY TO WIN THIS GAME

The first price is *pressure* of our wills, gentle but constant. What game is ever won without effort and concentration?

The second price is *perseverance*. A low score at the outset is not the least reason for discouragement; everybody gets a low score for a long while. Each week grows better and requires less strain.

The third price is *perfect surrender*. We lose Christ the moment our wills rebel. If we try to keep even a remote corner of life for self or evil, and refuse to let God rule us wholly, that small worm will spoil the entire fruit. We must be utterly sincere.

The fourth price is *tell others*. When anybody complains that he is losing the game, we flash this question back at him: "Are you telling your friends about it?" For you cannot keep Christ unless you give Him away.

The fifth price is *to be in a group*. We need the stimulus of a few intimate friends who exchange their experiences with us.

The Prizes We Win

It is obvious that this is unlike other games in many respects. One difference is that *we all win*. We may not win all or even half of our minutes but we do win a richer life, which is all that really matters. There are no losers except those who quit. Let us consider some of those prizes:

1. We develop what Thomas à Kempis calls a "familiar friendship with Jesus." Our Unseen Friend becomes dearer, closer, and more wonderful every day until at last we know Him as "Jesus, lover of my soul" not only in songs, but in blissful experiences. Doubts vanish, we are more sure of Him being with us than of anybody else. This warm, ardent friendship ripens rapidly until people see its glory shining in our eyes—and it keeps on growing richer and more radiant every month.

2. All we undertake is done better and more smoothly. We have daily evidence that God helps our work, piling one proof upon another until we are sure of God, not from books or preachers, but from our own experience.

3. When we are playing this game our minds are pure as a mountain stream every moment.

4. The Bible and Christian hymns seem like different books, for they begin to sparkle with the beautiful thoughts of saints who have had glorious experiences with God. We begin to understand their bliss for we share it with them.

5. All day long we are *contented*, whatever our lot may be, for He is with us. "When Jesus goes with me, I'll go anywhere."

6. It becomes easy to tell others about Christ because our minds are flooded with Him. "Out of the fullness of the heart the mouth speaketh."

7. Grudges, jealousies, hatred, and prejudices melt away. Little hells turn into little heavens. Communities have been transformed where this game was introduced. Love rises like a kindly sea and at last drowns all the demons of malice and selfishness. Then we see that the only hope

for this insane world is to persuade people to "practice the presence of God."

8. "Genius is 90 percent concentration." This game, like all concentration upon one objective, eventually results in flashes of new brilliant thought which astonish us, and keep us tiptoe with expectancy for the next vision which God will give us.

INFINITE VARIETY

The notion that religion is dull, stupid, and sleepy is abhorrent to God, for He has created infinite variety and He loves to surprise us. If you are weary of some sleepy form of devotion, probably God is as weary of it as you are. Shake out of it, and approach Him in one of the countless fresh directions. When our minds lose the edge of their zest, let us shift to another form of fellowship as we turn the dial of a radio. Every tree, every cloud, every bird, every orchestra, every child, every city, every soap bubble is alive with God to those who know His language.

It Is for Anybody

Humble folk often believe that walking with God is above their heads, or that they may "lose a good time" if they share all their joys with God. What tragic misunderstanding, to regard Him as a killer of happiness! A growing chorus of joyous voices round the world fairly sing that spending their hours with God is the most thrilling joy ever known, and that beside it a baseball game or a horse race is stupid.

Radiant Religion

This game is not a grim duty. Nobody need play it unless he seeks richer life. It is a delightful privilege. If you forget to play it for minutes or hours or days, do not groan or repent, but begin anew with a smile. It is a thrilling joy—don't turn it into a sour-faced penance. With God, every minute can be a fresh beginning. Ahead of you lie limitless anticipations. Walt Whitman looked up into the starry skies and fairly shouted.

Away, O Soul, hoist instantly the Sail!
O daring joy but safe!
Are they not all the seas of God?
O farther, farther, farther sail!

WHAT IT MEANS BY WINNING

You win your minute if during that minute you either

1. Pray.

2. Recall God.

3. Sing or hum a devotional hymn.

4. Talk or write about God.

5. Seek to relieve suffering of any kind in a prayerful spirit.

6. Work with the consciousness of God's presence.

7. Whisper to God.

8. Feel yourself encompassed by God.

9. Look at a picture or a symbol of Christ.

10. Read a scripture verse or poem about God.

11. Give somebody a helpful hand for the Lord's sake.

12. Breathe a prayer for the people you meet.

13. Follow the leading of the Inner Voice.

14. Plan or work for the Kingdom of God.

15. Testify to others about God, the church, or this game.

16. Share suffering or sorrow with another.

17. Hear God and see Him in flowers, trees, water, hills, sky.

We never attempt to keep a minute-by-minute record (except perhaps occasionally for an hour), since such a record would interfere with a normal life. We are practicing a new freedom, not a new bondage. We must not get so tied down to score keeping that we lose the glory of it, and its spontaneity. We fix our eyes upon Jesus, not upon a clock.

Frank C Laubach

BENTON, PENNSYLVANIA 1781

**FIRST DAY
ISSUE**
2 SEPTEMBER 1884

Biographical Information

Frank C. Laubach (September 2, 1884–June 11, 1970) was a Christian evangelical missionary and mystic known as "The Apostle to the Illiterates." A Pennsylvanian, Laubach trained at Princeton University, Union Theological Seminary, and Columbia University (where he attained a PhD in sociology in 1915). He went to the Philippines in 1915 as a missionary for the American Board of Foreign Missions.

In 1929, after fourteen years of successful teaching, writing, and administration in Cagayan and Manila, he pursued his long-standing ambition of settling among the fierce Moros, a Muslim tribe on Mindanao. There, in the province of Lanao, he underwent a remarkable series of experiences of God and simultaneously developed a technique for reducing the Moro language to writing with symbols closely correlated to their spoken words. This technique not only made it possible to teach them to read in only a few hours but also permitted them to teach others immediately.

In 1928, two years before his transforming experiences, Laubach found himself profoundly dissatisfied. He then realized in 1930 that after fifteen years as a Christian minister he was still not living his days "in minute-by-minute effort to follow the will of God." He determined at that time to seek to begin lining up his actions with the will of God every few minutes. His confidants at the time told him he was seeking the impossible. Undeterred, he began to try living all his waking moments in "conscious listening to the inner voice, asking without ceasing, 'What, Father, do you desire said? What, Father, do you desire done this minute?' " He believed that this was exactly what Jesus did every day.

Letters by a Modern Mystic, first published in 1937, is a compilation of excerpts from letters that Laubach wrote to his father. The tremendous results of this experiment in living in moment-by-moment communion with God are found in the narrative of these letters. *The Game with Minutes*, on page 85 of this book, is the practical guide Laubach developed to assist others in applying the principles articulated in his letters.

Dr. Laubach is probably best known for his work to address adult illiteracy in the world. He conceived a simple method of instruction that permitted even the most disadvantaged people in the world not only to learn to read but also to be able to teach others. "Each One Teach One" became the slogan for this instructional program, which is credited with equipping over one hundred million people with the ability to read. On September 2, 1984, the United States Postal Service issued a stamp commemorating the 100th anniversary of Laubach's birth.

Frank Laubach died in 1970 at the age of 85. His commitment to live in constant conscious communion with the Father not only transformed him personally but also permitted him to make a significant impact on illiteracy in the world, a work that continues today through ProLiteracy Worldwide, an organization he helped establish.